Love Looks Pretty on You

Also by Lang Leav

POETRY
Love & Misadventure
Lullabies
Memories
The Universe of Us
Sea of Strangers

FICTION
Sad Girls

Love Looks Pretty on You

Lang Leav

Andrews McMeel
PUBLISHING®

For Michael,
my love.

Andrews McMeel Publishing
a division of Andrews McMeel Universal
1130 Walnut Street, Kansas City, Missouri 64106

www.andrewsmcmeel.com

www.langleav.com

19 20 21 22 23 BVG 10 9 8 7 6 5 4 3 2 1

ISBN: 978-1-4494-9935-8

Library of Congress Control Number: 2018960375

This book is a work of fiction. Names, characters,
places, and incidents either are products of the author's
imagination or are used fictitiously. Any resemblance
to actual events or locales or persons, living or dead, is
entirely coincidental.

ATTENTION: SCHOOLS AND BUSINESSES
Andrews McMeel books are available at quantity
discounts with bulk purchase for educational, business, or
sales promotional use. For information, please e-mail the
Andrews McMeel Publishing Special Sales Department:
specialsales@amuniversal.com.

Introduction

Six is the highest roll on the die, the Lovers in a tarot deck, and Virgo in the zodiac.

My sixth poetry title, *Love Looks Pretty on You*, is a celebration of the female spirit. In this book I weave the threads of my past to complete the tapestry of my present. I reflect on my life to this point, as a woman and a creator who has come full circle.

In this book I pay homage to my mother and to my sisters, all over the world.

I celebrate the synergy of our work and relationships.

The love we have for each other and, most importantly, the love we have for ourselves.

Love looks pretty on you, and you should wear it with pride.

x Lang

At Last

Love looks pretty on you. Makes you soft, tender, proud.
Makes you sit up and take notice. Gives you a home to set
down your things.

What a blessing it is, to have music and dancing and poetry.
What a gift it is, to look at someone and say,

*I'm so happy to have found you—at last, at last, at long, long
last—you're here.*

All this time, I thought I was writing for the lovers, when I've been writing for the writers.

The Long Way

You're the girl who takes the long way home. This is the way you do it. This way you will have stories to tell. About lovers and liars, thieves and kings. You will have spine-chilling tales to spin.

You will see the ones who rose so fast, dazzled for a moment before they crashed back down to earth, crawled back into the dust.

But not you. Never you.

This is the way you've always been. A hook at the end of a long, long line. Waiting patiently. You will get there and believe me when you get there: you will be glad you took your time.

Don't stay where you are needed. Go where you are loved.

Making History

History will look back on critics
as one collective voice,
tainted with bitterness,
colored by their ignorance
and failure to find
the pulse of their generation.

As for the poets,
history will look back
and know us by name.

Endless Cycle

You want to hurt your father for all the times he has made your mother cry. Because you're the only one in the world he loves more than himself. So, in a weird, fucked-up way, you find yourself with someone just like him, and just like you wanted, you see the hurt in your father's eyes. But it ends up hurting you too.

And I can already picture us ten years from now, living our lives like parallel lines. Looking across at each other from time to time.

Someone Else

I don't think it's right, telling someone to stop needing somebody else. Have you ever felt the twist of loneliness in the pit of your stomach? Sat in silence with nothing to look forward to? The last thing you should do is tell someone they can fix it on their own. That no one else can fix it for them. Believe me, sometimes all it takes is someone else.

This Year

I am starting this year barefoot in the sand. Moonlight on my skin and sea-wind through my hair. Love in my heart and murder in my veins.

This is not the year I leave to chance or karma. It is not a year to live and let live.

If we have unfinished business, the wolves will be howling your name. If there is blood on your hands, you will get what you deserve.

If you think you're safe, all you've done is bought yourself time. If you think distance can protect you, I can cross oceans in a heartbeat.

And if ever you find my name slipping from your memory, I can promise you, by the time this year is through, you will never forget it again.

More or Less

When love is seen
from two points of view,
what we were
I can only guess.

I am certain it was love
with you—
but to love,
you did not confess.

So was it I—
Who made it more?
Or was it you—
Who made it less?

I have buried myself so deep in my words that sometimes I can't tell if I am the person writing or the one hiding between the lines.

My Mother

My mother was a woman
without country as I lay
curled in her womb.

Her body marked for death,
teeming with life. My life,
barely a glow when she
glared into the pit of darkness,

a hairline crack from death,
crawling to the light,
dreaming of a faraway shore,
and a little girl in her arms.

My mother, my safe passage
into this world, fought a war
to show me wars can be won.

How Love Leaves You

There is no telling how you will love when you do, if you will let it consume you or free you. If love is a chain-link fence or a pair of wings. If love comes on a Monday morning or a Sunday afternoon. Who knows what gifts or sorrows it will bring?

But we all know the story of how love leaves you, if you think back to when it last left. And if you've forgotten, let me remind you. How love never really ends. How your heart breaks the same way it beats, again and again, and again.

Vultures

We all have moments of darkness, moments when we are so unlike ourselves. And like vultures they wait for a slip, a misstep, then they take that part of us and try to convince the world that is all we are.

Pandora's Box

Longing has a language
that is all her own.
The language of skin,
the language of flowers.

I am a body of longing,
a vessel of language.

For you, I am calamity
in a locked box
where the key is still turning.

For you, I am a mistress
in her ivory tower humming.

For you, I am a songbird
preening her feathers.

For you, for you,
I am a bed of roses,
blooming.

Every time I see my name, I hear it in your voice.

Regrets

There it is, that one thing in your past you wish you could undo. It sits in your mind like a big, red, tantalizing bow. A gentle tug is all it would take to set things right.

If only you could get to it.

But you can't.

Letter to the Past

Tomorrow, you're going to fall in love, and it won't be pretty. Tell your mother, even though it will terrify her. Tell her you love him so much, that for once in your life, you don't have words for it. Tell her it hurts when he looks at you, when he takes from you. Tell her how the sun has betrayed you, how she only carries his light. When he isn't there, everything is a shadow of his absence.

Don't go upstairs with him. You're going to regret it. He'll never change. I know you're so lonely you can't stand it. The kind of lonely that has teeth. A lone wolf howling at the moon. There is a savagery to what you feel. It eats you up inside. But you will get through it; you don't need his mouth to placate you. You don't need his hands to untangle the butterfly knot in your heart. Your love is a fire that will burn itself out. Let it ravage you.

Things are coming you can't even imagine. If you knew what they were, you would forgive this one injustice, this one catastrophe that has brought your life to a screeching, screaming halt. The world will turn for you again, and when it does, it will take you anywhere you want.

I have to go now, but I love you. I need to leave you, but I'll always be with you. One day, you'll meet me here, and I will tell you this: I will tell you that we made it.

Loyalty

The only ones
they can turn
against you
are those
who were never
with you.

I Should Have Left You Then

In the glow of my eternal youth,
when I had yet to learn my truth;
in sun-soaked days I saw no end—
I should have left you then.

When my life felt like it wasn't mine,
and I knew I was running out of time;
that if I didn't leave, I'd never know—
I should have let you go.

When the world had yet its fill of me,
and there was so much left to see;
my love, I should have left you when,
there was time for me to start again.

I am in a tug-of-war with my past self. We're fighting over who gets to keep you.

Idols

You put her on a pedestal. Love her, adore her, crown her as your queen. Then you watch and wait, for a slip, a split second when her guard is down. You would tear her into pieces just to claim a fragment of her story.

No one can be perfect all the time. Why do you expect her to be any different? Why is she held to an impossible standard? Why do you take it so personally when she contradicts the version of herself that exists only in your head?

You think you know her, that she owes you somehow. That her existence is only relative to yours. But she is her own person. She lives and breathes, she hopes and dreams. She has a life, a love, a family, a purpose. And she doesn't owe anyone a damn thing.

Your Right to Love

It is your right to define love on your own terms. Love between two consenting adults is never wrong, no matter how much anyone tries to convince you it is.

Be with the person who makes you happy. Who makes your heart sing.

It is your right to endlessly curate your life.

Let her be herself. Or she will be somebody else's.

Wonder

The first thing you sent me were fireworks. Sparks of light and color over a bridge to nowhere. I was already in love when we met that summer; I belonged to someone else. To make room for you, I had to ask the world for permission, but every answer was a dead end. But who am I to blame them for telling me what I already knew?

So, I danced around you like a storm, white light against the cool black sky, like strobe lights flickering on and off. I said we could be something, you and me. I said so much and meant it, but never proved it to you, did I? We both know what my word was worth, you and me both.

You took my hand under a Ferris wheel, spitting light, spinning lies. You dazzled me, you know. You were incandescent. I don't think we could have been anything, not really. But isn't it something to wonder?

You turn him into poetry because you can't have him any other way.

Before

Before the dream is over,
before our lives are set—
before we're good and sober,
there's a chance now for us yet.

Before we grow too tired,
before our spirits wane;
let's leave the calm and quiet,
and never look back again.

Let's listen to the wise men,
throw caution to the wind—
to hell with a lifetime wondering
of all that could have been.

Let's take this golden moment,
and make a memory shine;
for all our days and always—
something that's yours and mine.

My Place

My heart is deeply rooted in the place I came from. At times I am ashamed, others I am proud.

In a single breath, I have gone from poverty to abundance.

I love the place I have come to. At times I am proud, others I am ashamed.

Sydney, 2007

Today I saw a photograph of the Argyle tunnel, projected with light, blooming with flowers, and it brought back a decade-old memory.

I was young and broken. But hopeful.

I was alone as I walked through the tunnel, my keys splayed between the fingers of my clenched fist in a makeshift weapon.

I was thinking, I should have left the party earlier. I was thinking, I should have asked someone to walk me to my car. I was thinking of the long drive ahead. I was thinking of the porch light my mother always left on for me.

As that girl, I couldn't see the future ahead. As the woman now, I can see it all. The pitfalls, the tragedies, the near misses and close calls, the years of wanting, waiting, wishing. The agony and beauty of my strange and twisted path.

I can see it all for her, as she is walking through that tunnel, not knowing what is waiting for her on the other side.

I wish I could tell her that we made it home.

Too Young

(Written at twelve years of age)

Too young for love
Too young to know
How far a touch
A kiss can go

Too old for comfort
Or childhood charms
Too old to be held
In my mother's arms

The world is hard
When you're in between
Your future world
And childhood dreams

Refugees

You don't think about life when you are living it, or love when you are loved. You don't think about hunger when there is abundance, or your dreams when they've come to fruition.

You think less about yourself and how you got to be here, and more about others who want to be where you are. And that's how it should be. Finding a place for yourself, then stretching your arms out to the rest of the world.

How do I thank my mother
for giving me the life
she desperately wanted
for herself?

What You Wish For

Change is the anthem of this year. For better. For worse. I am bracing myself for the crash, steeling myself for the fall. I am swimming in a sky-blue sea where I can't tell which way is up.

You know, I used to be a love letter, folding endlessly into myself. For your eyes only. Now I am torn into a thousand pieces, my soul a burst of confetti raining words onto the world.

Something tells me it's been a long time coming. Someone whispers, *Be careful what you wish for.* Because the heart can't retract what it once wanted. Didn't you know it is the universal law?

Now go back to the years you waited. All that time you spent yearning. *Be careful what you wish for.* It never comes the way you think.

Force a smile for the camera
Bite your tongue
You can taste blood in your mouth,
can't you?
Think of what you gave up to get here
You haven't eaten in days
Slept in fits and starts
Not even sure you want
what you're so afraid to lose
You can feel it can't you?
A metal spring twisting
through your body
A wind-up doll in fancy dress
A jack-in-the-box at every turn
What's next?
Your face on someone else's body
Someone else's words in your mouth
Your life is worth less
than their fifteen minutes
But that's the trap you set for yourself
Your freedom for this
Your peace of mind for this
Is it worth it?

I Had You

Last night I had a dream that felt like a memory. A glimpse of what could have been. Crossed signals from another life.

Where instead of all this, I had you.

And life was exquisitely simple. And we were desperately happy.

Her Crown

Another thing
she did,
they said
she couldn't do.
Another jewel
in her crown.

The Friendship Bond

There is that one friend whom you no longer speak to, who is no longer part of your life. If you saw them across the street, you would turn your head away and they would do the same.

But if they ever called you in the middle of the night, you would be there for them, sure as the sun. And you know that if you were the one to make that call, no matter how much time has passed or how distant you've become, they would be there for you.

He only wants you
when he can't have you.
So why don't you give him
what he wants.

I have been quiet lately, I know. Not because I don't have anything to say, but because I have too much.

Slut Shaming

Misogyny is like a malignant virus, the way it seeps into your life and puts you in a position of painful vulnerability. Where even the people who love you will judge you for your past. Where the act of sex degrades a woman and celebrates a man. The infuriating double standard where a man will admire a girl in a string bikini, and in the same breath, tell his partner that her skirt is too short.

When my best friend told me
she was in love
my first thought was,
I hope he is good to her.

And it suddenly occurred to me,
what I held in my heart for her
was hope, when it should
have been expectation.

If we were together, we'd still miss each other. And that's the reason why we're not.

Twenty-Seven

What age are you when you dream about yourself. In the thick, underwater flashes of coherence not knowing you're asleep. I am twenty-seven and the drawer has just slammed shut on my hand. And I have yet to know pain—raw and undulating—I have yet to know loss, the kind that strips you back from yourself, makes you over into something else.

In my dreams, there are photographs of me that don't exist. And I am backlit against the sun, face in shadow, hair bathed in golden light. The fabric of my subconscious looks for you, calls to you, a fisherman and his net, coming up empty. And you wear the face of someone I loved, at twenty-seven. And my heart is like the ocean, breaking like waves, breaking all throughout the ages.

In the wrong hands, your past is a weapon.

First Steps

While you look at yourself through someone else's eyes, you are not free.

If you speak the words that have come from someone else's mouth, you are not free.

When you say yes when your heart is screaming no, you are not free.

There are things we sacrifice for love, that we willingly give. But no one who loves you will ever ask you to give up more than you are willing.

Someone who has your heart is not entitled to your body. No one lays a finger on you without your permission.

No one makes you feel ashamed for knowing the people you've known. Or loving the people you've loved. Do not allow someone to undermine your past to appease their ego.

While you continue to compromise who you are, for the sake of another, you are not free.

When you find yourself compensating for someone else's insecurities, you are not free.

If you find yourself worrying when you have done nothing wrong, you are not free.

First, you must recognize you are not free. Say it out loud to yourself. *I am not free.* Tell someone who cares about you. *I am not free.*

This is the first step you have taken back to yourself.

Flowers

Somewhere in the midst of celebration, the roar of applause, the bright, glittering jewel of her triumph, she felt lacking.

Yet, alone in her garden, barefoot in the dirt, a moment so ordinary it should not have left an impression, should have come and gone without so much as a thought—she felt a surge of joy that warmed her so unexpectedly, so completely—it was as though it had been waiting for her all this time.

Waiting among the flowers.

Now that you have it all, do you ever wish you could go back
to when you had it simple?

Love's Train

Love's train arrived on platform one,
pulled in, pulled out, and then was gone.
The carriages bursting at the seams,
held within their doors—a dream.

And though they opened invitingly,
and every face had turned to me.
Sadly, I saw, without a doubt—
not a single soul walked in or out.

How many people have we known all our lives, and never once loved. How many people have we loved, and never known.

One day a moment will come to you.
And you will live every day of your life,
with this moment.

It will come
and it will go—
it will go before you are ready.

And its memory will feel more real to you
than the moment you lived it,

and this moment has a life
that is separate from yours
yet is wholly belonging.

It will come
and it will go—
it will go before you are ready.

And for the first time
you will learn what it is
not to be ready.

You are a writer bleeding words onto a page. And the ones who hate you will trample on that page. And the ones who love you will cut you, to keep you bleeding.

The novelist struggles.
The poet suffers.

Saltwater

The poet stands
before the ocean
like an offering
takes off her clothes,
peels off her skin.
Keeps stripping herself back,
until she is only heart and pulse;
blood and saltwater.

And she cries,
My body can't hold
this much.

And the tears spill
down her cheeks
like a person drowning.

The poet puts out her hands,
and cups the ocean,
then lets it go.

A Love Letter to Bali

I will never forget those slow, languid days, warm and balmy. The sun was a pomegranate red, ripe, and full of promise, painting the sky pink. We stayed in a Grecian-style villa, overlooking the shoreline, watching the waves crash onto the lazy stretch of sand below.

The daylight sunk into starlight like a slow transition, as we lost track of time altogether. My skin grew luminous and shone from the inside, glowed like a lantern. White crescent moons appeared at the bottom of my fingernails. My hair grew thicker, wilder. We were feasting on exotic fruits and midnight conversations that drifted into the sea salt breeze.

We slept. We woke up in the half-light to watch the sun come up. We didn't write a single word.

Mischievous monkeys scampered across our balcony. Frogs hopped in our path and out of sight again, the sound of their croaking ever-present. Tiny birds darted in and out of our line of vision like thoughts.

The half-moon yawned when we waved goodbye to another moment, lost to memory. The walls learned our secrets like how you like your coffee black and I like mine with cream and sugar. We left something of ourselves behind.

He feels like the culmination of every good deed I've done.

Shut Out

I felt it every day, that feeling of exclusion. Like a gradual drop in temperature. A slow freezing out of a world I once belonged to. I was nudged ever so slowly toward the exit, I didn't even see the door. I only realized it was too late when I found myself standing outside.

Never Again

You will come back to me many times over,
as a flower,
a white cat,
the king of hearts in a deck.

You will come to me
as love,
as a symbol of it,
as a lover I'll regret
or a dear friend I knew I'd wronged.

You will come back to me
as a lesson,
a song,
a star-shaped birthmark
on the cheek of a beautiful stranger.

You will come back to me again and again
in your shape-shifter clothes and you'll hold
your breath and wait for me to see through
your disguise, to catch you out and smile
your secret back at you knowing, like the sun,

you'll always come back,
in a multitude of miracles,
you'll always come back,
like the memory of September,
you'll always come back

but never, never again as yourself.

The most beautiful thing is not when you learn to live without something; it's the moment you realize you never needed it in the first place.

Woman's Anthem

Women are fierce. They are powerful. No matter what language they speak, how they dress, or the work they choose to do. What matters is they have a choice, and the freedom to carve out a life for themselves.

As long as we know women who are strong and resilient, we must respect them, carry them forward, lift them up.

For they are the product of all our other selves, the women we were, the ones we strive to be, the collective struggle of our mothers, our sisters, our daughters.

Our salvation will only come if we stand together.

Be patient. Your voice will find its way into the world, not in one loud instance but a steady trickle that turns into a deluge.

It Was Love

It was the mood of the time, the feeling of forever. The sense we could live and die by our word and never regret a thing.

You were so in love with everything when I walked into your life, all I wanted was to be part of that.

But you couldn't say it was love, could you?

You couldn't say it wasn't, either.

Gold

He carries around
a piece of her history
like loose change
not knowing one day,
everything she's touched
will turn into gold.

Abusive Relationships

There is a knot of injustice that sits in your stomach. You know how you are being treated is wrong, but you don't know how to word it. And even if you could put it into words, you don't know how to make people listen. And the only one who will listen, is the one who is responsible for your suffering. And the only one who understands you, is the one who undermines you. And your abuser has created a world where the volume is turned all the way down so even if you ever found your voice, no one would hear it.

Trapped

I believed he loved me in his way,
the scars I needn't show—
there was nowhere else to go.

I said I was happy to be his girl,
if only I had known—
my words were not my own.

Universal law dictates that not a soul can hurt you without first handing you the keys to their own destruction.

True Love

I have walked side by side with loss. I have laid my head down on his lap and felt his palm against my cheek. It is true; I have been intimate with loss.

I have invited him into my heart, into my bed.

I have let him live with me for all this time.

And it was only after having known him, did I understand: he is an intermediary, a bridge to something much more beautiful.

For it is only through my meeting with loss, that I can truly know love.

The Gift of Everything

You were the bearer of heartache,
of pain, like nothing I had ever known.

But look at what I have because of you.
Look at what I've built.

Only now can I look back
and recognize the gift
you have given me.

Only now can I look at the
all-consuming beauty of my life,
press my palm to yours and say,
Thank you for the gift of everything.

Rebirth

I tried to keep the wanting
from my voice when I said,

I can't become without you,

and he whispered thickly,
open up for me, my little orchid,
I will put my mouth wherever it hurts,

and I couldn't give a name
to the ache blooming in my chest,
couldn't think of the word,

flower.

This Was the Year

This was the year I didn't see coming—the one that shook me out of complacency. When I learned to stop being compliant, to demand what was rightfully mine, refuse to settle for anything less than what I deserved.

I lost patience with small talk, fell in love with midnight conversations. I crossed deserts and oceans with the man I love at my side, as we lived out of suitcases, drunk on life and laughter.

This was the year that came with a gentle tap on the shoulder, reminding me who I was and what I could be, if only I'd just open my arms and let the light in, stop overthinking and start living. Give myself permission to fall as long as I got back up again.

I held the ones I love closer—let go of the things that weren't meant to be mine. Looked my past dead in the eye and said, *You aren't welcome here anymore.* Chased away the cobwebs that I had let linger far too long. Told the moon I was sorry, but this is now my time in the sun.

Time goes by and your world gets so much smaller. Your heart grows so much bigger.

I Know Love

I know love now because I am in love. Because of how long I've loved. Because of the man I love.

Love used to be a beautiful mirage, a moonbeam on the water I tried to cup in my hands. Now it is a grand oak tree, tried and tested, roots driving deep down into the earth. I have a love that takes me across oceans. A love that tells me I am home, no matter where I am in the world.

From My Heart

I bit my tongue
when I heard the words
that came out of my mouth,
the expression on your face,
the hurt.

If I said another thing,
it couldn't fix it,
so, I will stay quiet now
and hope somewhere deep down,
you get that my words
may not have been
in the right place
but my heart was.

What He's Lost

Promise me something. You are going to show him what he's giving up. Even if it takes your whole life, you will make sure that day will come. Until then, you are going to do amazing things. That fire in your belly will set the world alight, while he watches from the sidelines, until all at once— the realization hits him like a punch in the gut—the weight of what he's lost.

Reflection

Everyone is trying to get to themselves, trying to get to the bare bones of who they are, what they stand for, where they draw the line. The thing is, you only get there by living—by screaming, laughing, crying, shaking, by letting go, one finger at a time. You get there by loving someone so much it makes you inexplicably cruel, by hurting a friend and only knowing the pain you caused when the same is done to you.

You come home to yourself when you have a thing or two to tell your past, when you see with crystal clarity the parts of yourself you need to keep or discard. You see the multitude of paths you could have taken, the things you could have seen. And you close your eyes, relieved and grateful that you ended up as you—out of all the people you could have been.

What is the part of you that you can't stand? How do you hide it and who are you most afraid will find out?

Anxiety

I struggle with things that are as easy to others as breathing.

Like breathing. Like answering the phone. Or sending that email I have been meaning to for weeks.

I panic when I am asked out to dinner, even if it's with someone I really want to see.

It's hard for me to commit to anything, and when I do, I overthink it until my brain tells me I have made a mistake, like a rat caught in a maze, trying to claw its way out.

I don't know why I am like this. People ask me why I can't do anything without jumping through a thousand thoughts, like hoops. But sometimes I wonder if my inability to function in the real world is really such a bad thing. I wonder if that's why I've spent so much time sheltered in my imagination.

And because I can't live in the real world, I create worlds to belong to. And I wonder if the very thing I've always been told is my weakness, has all along, been my strength.

Obsession

I want to cut your name in half
with a scalpel, join the first
to mine; stitch the second
into the sleeve of my sweater.

I want to wear you like skin,
hold you hard against me
while I think up a checklist
of the things I would surrender.

I am more you than I am myself
these days, more you than you;
I see what you see, when you look
at me, my own eyes looking back.

A Meeting of Selves

On a long, empty road I was walking, I met my future self.
Her hair, white as snow, hung down to her hips, with eyes
that carried the wisdom of a sage. She pointed at the city
behind me, the one I'd left crumbling into dust, and she said,

*There is our past self among the ruins. She, the girlish one, the
foolish one, the one who longs for a place with us here, where she is
not welcome. The one who seeks to undo what we've done. She is
chaos and ego. She knows only darkness and destruction.*

She unfurled her fists, palms pointed in my direction.

*And here you are, our present self, a woman in bloom, a picture of
temperance, regard for kindness and humility. You have a strength
that carries your entire life and the life of others. Knowledge of
something sacred has changed and shaped you in a myriad of ways.*

Then, she lifted her chin and her gaze penetrating mine,
reflected the depths of her sincerity. *And what you must now
understand is the two of you should never be allowed to meet.*

The Present

You are here. Safe in the knowledge you are unequivocally happy. That you always were, even when you had nothing. Your soul sings with gratitude for the peace you have found. The love you have found. For the quiet that allows you to do your work and still find time.

Time to watch the flowers grow, time to watch the children grow. Time for everything that is still to come.

I don't think about myself as much as I used to. I guess that's a good thing. I only think about the things that are missing from me.

More Than You

When have you known me not to go for what I wanted? To chase it down like hail and thunder. Move heaven and earth to get a beat closer.

So, if I've stopped calling, don't kid yourself. It's not because I'm afraid of getting hurt again. It's because I have found something I want more than you.

Youth

You're young and there's still so much ahead. So much uncertainty and doubt. It keeps you up at night—this wild, restless feeling. But you don't know how free you are. For this short, miraculous time, you have no one to answer to, nothing to lose. You belong wholly to yourself. And even though some days you wish your world would stop spinning for a second, to let you catch your breath—believe me, someday you're going to look back on this and you're going to miss this feeling.

Here's the story of my life. Hoping they would care about me or wishing they wouldn't care so much.

How Love Comes and Goes

I felt a void within me—
It was vast as the desert plains.
It could swallow up the seven seas
And hardly notice the gain.

I felt this emptiness echo
On the day, my love, you came.
When love swept in like the ocean
And left me in drops, like rain.

Looking for Love

Everything looks wrong, if you look at it long enough. A word so familiar to you, one you know back to front, will suddenly feel alien if you keep staring at it. So, do not look too much at love. Do not give it another thought. Love is one of those things that will happen to you when you are not looking.

These Years

These are the years that have come at me from nowhere, from nothing, before I was ready. Before I knew how to give as good as I get.

They have come in a rush, a whirlwind, joy dressed as hardship, happiness cloaked in sorrow, sunshine overflowing in my cupped palms.

These years have come as a trial, a lesson, a fire lit within me that cannot be diminished, a beautiful dream and the will to see it through.

I am thankful for these years, to be humbled by them, to let them do what they will, and I count my blessings day by day, count the years that follow, knowing I will make them mine.

There are days when I don't see you, touch you, hear you. But not a day goes by where I don't feel you.

Sunday Afternoon

We keep each other
while the lilacs bloom outside,
while coffee spills like inkblots
on bone white sheets.

We keep each other like cats,
lazy and warm stretched by the fire,
like secrets told in the dead of night.
We keep each other in love and light,

in our darkest hour,
we keep each other safe.

Why You Fell in Love

You said you never wanted a girl like me, that I was too much. You said being with me was like looking right into the sun. But I don't know how to be what you want, when this is why you wanted me in the first place. The very thing you want to change about me is the reason why you fell in love.

Something Else

It's impossible for me to feel just one emotion at a time. Even in moments of pure, unadulterated joy, there is always an intrusion of something else, a pinprick of guilt or sorrow shaped by a voice, not quite my own, telling me *I don't deserve this*.

Your Name

To speak a word about you,
my lips do not dare.
Yet my pen flows on without you,
my mouth, it holds a prayer.

Some days I am better,
others, I sit and dwell.
How much can the heart weather?
This, I cannot tell.

For the storm is far from over,
this, I learn day by day;
love is a weight you shoulder—
it is how I carry your name.

Elements

I am contrary, like the weather.
I change my mind,
from moment to moment.
Something I once believed in,
I no longer do.
But when I did,
I felt it with all my sincerity.

I am made of the elements,
ever changing.

A forest fire to a candle flame.
A breeze to a hurricane.
A handful of dirt
to a mountaintop.
An ocean to a raindrop.

Anyone in Love

In the past, you spoke to me about the future. Painted a picture of our lives, in light and shade. Told me you would always take care of me and in your own way, you have. But first, you had to break my heart.

If you have wondered about me, know that I am doing fine. I don't have a stitch of ill will toward you, despite the way it ended. I know you were finding your way. I know you had to lose me to do it.

I don't think we found each other at the wrong time, because there was so much that was right about it. We gave each other something you couldn't name—that anyone in love would know.

The less you speak, the more weight your words will carry when you do.

House of Straw

Women, build your house, while you are young. When your shoulders can carry the world. Before the weight of children and men. Build your house. Not with needles and haystacks. Not with wood and sticks. Not with matches and straw. Build your house with bricks.

Protect yourself from the wind and the wolves. Arm yourself with nails. Paper and pen. Hang your name on your door. Only then are you safe in the house you built—your house of bricks—when this house you built is yours.

Write for Yourself

You want to write for the world but you can't figure out what the world wants.

If you write for a trend, it'll be over before you can get a word out. If you write for fame and fortune, your work will lack authenticity.

So, remember, writing is a journey inward, not out.

Write for the simple joy of knowing your own thoughts.

Write for yourself.

That is what the world wants.

There will come a time when your journey will matter less than imparting what you've learned to those who wish to follow in your footsteps.

Unforgiven

I believe in forgiveness, in wishing those well who have hurt me. But I'm going to make you an exception. Because the truth is, I hope to God you suffer every heartache you put me through. I hope when the darkness comes for you, it will hit you twice as hard as it hit me. And I hope you will curse my name, knowing I was the one who sent it.

Wolves

Who will protect me with you gone? Who will keep the wolves from the door while I sleep? My love, you are my shelter, my strength, my shield. Before you, I have held my own, I am a force in my own right. But you are my superpower. And, now that I have known life with you, how can I ever be without?

My Heart and Time

I love you in the way that not a single word comes to me, without sounding like hope. I love your hands, not quite sure, and your curious, candid eyes. What I miss more than anything is your laughter. Like memory, it cuts through anything. Through my heart and time.

Love and Loss

There is no such love that can hold you
without you first withholding love.

No love that can bind you, until you've
known love that knows no bounds.

Love is what makes living worthwhile—
a measure of what your life is worth.

Love comes to you with loss as its shadow
to remind you of what you could lose

Springtime

Morning light, leafy Sunday,
the sun comes pouring in.
I rouse from you a waking smile
so my day can begin.

Down the street for a coffee,
I stop to pick up the news;
I stop for milk and flowers
And take them home to you.

Do you know that cherries
have come into season?
The air feels light and warm,
perhaps you are the reason.

You greet me by the doorway,
birdsong fills the room—
my love, look out the window,
our garden's come into bloom.

At the core of love is strength, and in its center is the quiet constant of your inner voice.

The one that no one hears but you.

Yet everyone can see, by the way you carry yourself in a crowded room. The power in how you use your words—the only thing you have ever loved in one continuous line.

A line that runs alongside your life.

And lives to tell your story.

In the only way that you know how.

I want to be someone without things. Untethered and boundless. To move gently through this world, without owing or owning. Take only the things I need and give back what I don't.

Live my life twice over.

And love my life for once.

For the Moon

For years I have written for the sun.
But tonight, I write for the moon.
I write to the part of myself
left in shadow;
the part I've kept hidden
for someone who loves me,
and is afraid of the truth.
For someone who loved me
for who I was;
I write for the moon.

My mother tells me to stay in the light;
it's not too late to change who you are.
She doesn't know what I think about
when the sun goes down,
and the night calls to me.

I think about rewriting the book.
Tempting the hand of fate.
I think about giving it all up
for a shot at something
I'm not even sure I want.

A Long Time Ago

Everything feels sentimental these days, every song feels loaded, feels somehow directed at me. Every emotion is heightened tenfold, your fingertips leaving burn marks on my skin.

I think it only feels this way for me when things are beginning or when they're ending.

And my love, we started this a long time ago.

Index

Acknowledgments

Al Zuckerman, what a treat it was to visit you and your wife, Claire, in New York. You've been nothing but supportive throughout my writing career, and I am truly grateful our paths crossed.

Kirsty Melville, can you believe this is our sixth poetry book together? (Looking forward to our second novel too!) Thank you for championing poetry and playing such a huge part in making it cool again.

Patty Rice, every book we've worked on has been so much fun! Thank you for the creativity and inspiration. I'll always think of us in LA with our husbands, laughing under the palm trees.

Kathy Hilliard, I had such a blast Ubering around NYC with you. Thank you for your hard work and dedication to this movement.

A big thank you to Jess Cruickshank and Diane Marsh, who worked on the gorgeous cover, and gg for, once again, lending us your beautiful art.

Michael and Ollie, the last ten years with you have been my happiest. The best is yet to come!

My readers, thank you for all the love and support you continue to show me. I am so blessed to have you. A million kisses.

About the Author

Novelist and poet Lang Leav was born in a Thai refugee camp when her family was fleeing the Khmer Rouge regime. She spent her formative years in Sydney, Australia, in the predominantly migrant town of Cabramatta. Among her many achievements, Lang is the winner of a Qantas Spirit of Youth Award, Churchill Fellowship, and Goodreads Choice Award. Aside from her success in publishing, Lang is an accomplished artist, having exhibited her work in Australia and the United States. She was one of twenty contemporary artists handpicked to exhibit in the landmark *Playboy Redux* curated by The Andy Warhol Museum and Playboy Enterprises.

Her first book, *Love & Misadventure* (2013), was a breakout success and, according to *Publishers Weekly,* foretold the poetry movement that is currently taking the publishing world by storm. Her subsequent books, including her debut novel, *Sad Girls*, continue to top bestseller charts worldwide. Lang actively participates in international writers' festivals, and her tours consistently draw massive crowds. With a combined social media following of two million, Lang's message of love, loss, and female empowerment continues to resonate with her multitude of readers.

Lang has been featured in various publications including the *Sydney Morning Herald*, the *Straits Times*, the *Guardian*, and the *New York Times*. She currently resides in New Zealand with her partner and fellow author Michael Faudet.

Join Lang Leav on the following:

Facebook   Twitter   Instagram   Tumblr